WHAT YOU SAY IS
What You Are

Activity Guide

Mission: To Proclaim Transformation and Truth

Publisher: Transformed Publishing, Cocoa, FL

Website: www.transformedpublishing.com

Email: transformedpublishing@gmail.com

ISBN: 978-1-953241-56-6

WHAT YOU SAY IS
What You Are
Activity Guide
Dr. Tanya Small, EdD

Dedication

Written for Timster, Tyke, RJ,
my nieces and nephews,
and all my students.

- Believe in yourself,
as Coach believes in you.
I am committed to your success.

Character Circle Featured Testimonials

I just finished reading the book, *What You Say Is What You Are*, by Dr. Small, and wow what a fantastic message to give to children. It builds self-esteem that so many of our children do not receive. It took us several days to read the complete book due to our busy schedule. Some children were so interested they came in the next two days with money to purchase the book for themselves. I was so excited! The children learned that they could create their own destiny by being positive about themselves. We will all remember and understand the message of the bird: *What You Say Is What You Are!*

-1st Grade Teacher
Forest Hill Elementary

Double-Dutch! Can you imagine students trying out for this? Not easy to do. They all want to be part of this and practice and prepare using visualization techniques they learned throughout the program. The students want it so badly they are motivated and amenable to the coaching. Journal writing is part of this and tracks how they feel during each practice and what it takes to reach their goal. When the students express their thoughts on paper things seem to make more sense to them or if they must find a solution by seeing it on paper, they usually try something else. It is through this challenge those individuals have learned problem-solving techniques as an additional bonus.

-ESE Teacher

It's an innovative program designed to help students reach new heights.

-Elementary School Principal

The program has made a difference at our school. Even in kindergarten, the students are excited about doing their best! The book, *What You Say Is What You Are*, has a good story that even kindergarten students can understand. It teaches the children to give themselves positive messages and this will help them do better in school. It made a difference in our school. All the teachers received copies of the book for the students to read independently or the teacher could read it aloud. It has great meaning for the children in many ways. The words, "If I believe it, then I will achieve it", has such a powerful meaning to the students. Now they know they can be or do anything as long as they believe.

-Kindergarten Teacher

President Obama appreciates hearing about the work and new ideas of people and organizations across the country. Thank you for contacting us.

-Special Assistant to the president and director of Presidential Correspondences

Congratulations! Please accept our appreciation for the dedication and superior skills exhibited and for your commitment to education and the children in Palm Beach County.

-Superintendent

The program was instrumental during the state testing in encouraging positive thinking during a stressful time. It was wonderful to see children in all grades giving each other a "thumbs up" sign to encourage each other to be "all they can be."

-Kindergarten Teacher

PROJECT DESCRIPTION:

Welcome:

Thank you for choosing the *What You Say Is What You Are,* Mentor Text and Activity Guide. This Activity Guide is designed to be implemented in small groups (within the classroom, community, or at home) to help children discover self-efficacy, build academic competence, and be empowered learners. This curriculum is intentionally divided into short lessons that build upon one another to ensure the principles are clearly established, practiced, and reinforced. It is recommended that this Activity Guide is facilitated using **Character Circles**.

What is a Character Circle?

A **Character Circle** is a group of students and a guide who come together, sitting in a circle, to examine themselves in terms of their habits, self-perception, and beliefs, pertaining to academic success. It's a place where participants come face-to-face with who they are as individuals. A place where they are empowered with the knowledge of how to be the best they can be one day at a time.

In the Character Circle participants learn vital life lessons that build self-confidence and boost enthusiasm towards learning and life. Participants learn how to program their habits, characteristics, self-concept, and beliefs for success. Character Circles give participants a voice through the *Power of Self-Talk*. Sessions can be facilitated in as little as 15 minutes (up to 1 hour).

Character Circles were birthed from this belief:

Students want to succeed.

More students would succeed if they just knew *how*. There are secrets to success that are unique to each individual student. The main **objective** is to empower students to discover the keys to unlocking their greatest academic potential. Students learn *how* to uncover the secrets to become a smarter, more intelligent learner:

- ✓ **How** to stimulate their intellect and empower their mind.
- ✓ **How** to succeed in school and in life.
- ✓ **How** to achieve academic success from the inside out.

Character Circles uniquely teach students these keys. The *What You Say Is What You Are,* Activity Guide ties character education to academic achievement. This program places the student in the driver seat by opening their eyes to self-efficacy.

What does it look like?

Step 1: Initiation (1 min.)
A group of children and a guide come together and sit in a circle. Each student has a *What You Say Is What You Are*, Mentor Text, Activity Guide, a writing tool, and a mirror (optional). The guide has the Character Chant audio and a compatible device to play it from. To begin, the guide states the Character Circle Lesson objective for the day.

Step 2: Presentation (4 min.)
The guide reads a particular section from the Activity Guide and engages the students with present-day examples and coping skills. The guide pauses to allow the participants to enter their private responses in their Activity Guide. The guide reminds the students to be honest with their responses since they are never required to share their entries. The guide continues by commenting on the possible responses of the participants, always favorably focusing on individualism.

Step 3: Core Discussion (10 min.)
The guide invites volunteers to share their entries, opinions, or comments throughout the session. The guide comments on each response with personal and relevant experiences. Here selected participants may share their past experiences or encounters with the specific subject area.

Step 4: Positive Affirmation (2 min.)
The guide extends an invitation for each participant to make a public positive statement to themself, while looking directly into the mirror. Participants who choose not to share may simply request to pass with absolutely no repercussions. Participants may share any positive self-affirmation statements. For example, "I am a winner because I always try my best. I will pass my classes and go to the next grade. I know that I can achieve all my goals." Initially, the students may imitate each other's statements. After each affirmation, the guide says, "I believe you will." or, "I can see you reaching that goal." etc. The guide also makes a positive affirmation, which may focus on a goal yet to be reached. (Toward the middle of the school year, most participants will be willing to share.)

Step 5: Overview (1 min.)
The guide summarizes the objectives of the session and explains to the students how they can tie what they have learned in with the real world and classroom environment to achieve success in any situation.

Step 6: Character Chant (2 min.)
The guide leads participants into the Character Chant (while playing the Character Chant audio from their compatible device). The students may tap their hands on their thighs to the rhythm and sing along.

Step 7: Conclusion (30 sec.)

The guide requests for each participant to make a positive statement to two other participants and dismisses the session. The session is almost exclusively unscripted, apart from the Activity Guide short reading sections.

During each session, the students successfully program their habits, self-concept, self-perception, and beliefs for success, by speaking positive affirmations into a mirror, as well as reciting a unique confidence-building chant. All cultures are equal, with no one 'in charge'. Free expression is encouraged in this non-threatening environment.

Projected Timeline:

In the classroom setting, each *Phase* represents approximately one month, because of time restraints. In the community or household setting, you may move through the *Phases* more quickly.

Phase 1: The *What You Say Is What You Are,* Mentor Text should be read prior to beginning the Activity Guide. It is integrated through the Activity Guide and is the main core reading selection for each lesson. The students explore the author's purpose and the theme.

Phase 2: Using the Activity Guide, students explore how their self-esteem, self-concept, and perception determine their emotions and their desire to try. They also learn about rational vs. irrational thinking and beliefs and identify their personal habits and practices as they relate to their beliefs about their abilities.

Phase 3: Students typically begin to understand self-efficacy and realize *their* personal role in their academic success.

Phase 4: Students continue to reinvestigate self-esteem issues and use positive affirmations as a means to motivate themselves and build efficacy.

Phase 5: Students embrace efficacy and begin to take ownership of their academic success.

Phase 6: Students' confidence levels soar as they begin to develop a new self-perception.

Phase 7: Students begin to embrace their unique culture and develop ethnic pride.

Phase 8: Lessons focus on guest speakers from the community, who have attained success despite of some form of a disparity or disability.

Phase 9: This is an exciting time in the program. Students begin to host the sessions, demonstrating their understanding of the concept and keys to success. In addition, they begin a designated ten-week challenge. During this period, they must believe they will achieve, speak daily positive self-affirmations, practice daily, and maintain a journal of each day's experiences. This is to prove that any skill that is practiced can be mastered. *The students may perform the special challenging skill in the school's annual talent show or a community / household gathering.

Phase 10: Students come to Character Circle with great enthusiasm. The focus is on building personal foundations about who they are, what they believe, and how they plan to achieve their goals.

Why incorporate a character circle?

BECAUSE OF THE PROBLEM:
Many students have created a mental block that even the most effective teachers with the best strategies have a hard time penetrating. From experience, a student who believes that he/she cannot beat another student in a race won't even attempt to win, and in fact will refuse to even enter the race. It's sad to say that some average students would prefer to fail from not trying than to have tried and failed. Herein lies the problem, "Because the brain cannot challenge the individual; the individual has to challenge his or her brain."

BECAUSE OF THE QUESTION:
How can a student who constantly tells themself, "I'm stupid and dumb. I can't win. I'm gonna fail. I'm a loser and there's nothing special about me," perform with confidence academically or otherwise?

BECAUSE OF THE SOLUTION:
Strategies are useless when thrown at a wall. The first step is to get the learner to remove the mental wall and embrace self-efficacy. Only then, will strategies become effective.

BECAUSE OF THE BENEFITS TO STUDENTS:
The Character Circle project will *benefit* all students involved. When students understand *why* they fail, they can take action toward success. Today, the average student enters the learning environment with severe complexes, which include low self-esteem issues, poor self-perception, and irrational beliefs about their abilities. These complexes result in the development of a 'fear of failure' - mental security wall, which is very difficult to penetrate. These students are obliviously caught in a pattern or cycle of learned helplessness and refuse to try. They will most likely be labeled as low achievers and give up unless they experience the Character Circle.

Why incorporate a character circle? Because truly, *'No Child Should Be Left Behind'*. Learning improves once students come face-to-face with the 'Power of Positive Affirmation' and learn they can program their mind to succeed. Participants learn that they fail or succeed because of the way they have programmed their brain. Informing students that their brain is as capable as any other brain, and that the difference between success and failure is simply 'practice', unleashes a power within them. Participants discover that their brain is as capable as any other brain. In addition, they learn how to reprogram the mind to succeed using such positive referent statements as, "I can! I will! I believe! I am a winner!"

More students would succeed if they just knew how. All students should be aware of their learning style, as well as the habits and practices, which contribute to failure. They should be taught how to study and organize information. Remember, strategies are useless when they are thrown against a wall. Therefore, students must learn *how* to remove the mental wall and embrace self-efficacy. Once the participants become aware of the practices, which hinder their success, they are then able to take action to remove those hindrances. Students become self-driven and develop intrinsic motivation, which results in increased test scores.

Character Circles impact students, parents, teachers, and communities in a positive way by equipping students with the characteristics to become great achievers and favorable members of society. Teachers and parents are amazed at the awakening of students who previously refused to try. The effectiveness of Character Circles is evaluated by various official assessments, direct observation of the students' attitudes toward learning and pre and post attitudinal tests.

PROGRAM EVALUATION:
The main objective is to empower students to discover the keys to unlocking their greatest academic potential. The effectiveness of this objective is evaluated by various official assessments, which indicate increased scores, of any degree. Another objective is for students to learn *how* to uncover secrets to become a smarter more intelligent learner. The effectiveness of this objective is evaluated by direct observation of the students' attitude toward learning and pre and post attitudinal tests. Additional evaluations entail observing new habits and practices, witnessing new self-concepts and motivation, and hearing new positive self-affirmations. Last but not least, mastering the *big challenge* provides a huge indication that the essence of the program has been internalized by the students.

What can be expected from a successful character circle?

1. Participants will begin to speak positively.
2. Participants, including those with specific learning difficulties, will begin to attempt to achieve.
3. Participants will begin to believe that they can succeed.
4. Self-esteem and efficacy will increase.
5. Most participants will be willing to share positive affirmations in the mirror halfway through the program.
6. Participants will begin to develop the understanding that being smart is an achievable goal.

7. Participants will demonstrate good character.

8. Participants will not absorb negative statements.

ROLE OF THE GUIDE:

The guide simply *guides* the session, to keep the discussion focused on the objective. All participants are equal, and no one is in charge. The guide too is a participant who shares, responds, and expresses. When a participant begins to go off track, the guide discretely ties the comment into the main objective and thanks the participant for sharing.

RESPONDING TO PARTICIPANTS' COMMENTS:

It is important to remember that a guide is not expected to take on the responsibilities of a guidance counselor or a school psychologist. A guide is still responsible to report all forms of child abuse if they suspect it based on a participant's response; moreover, the guide is not encouraged to pry further into any comment made by a student who appears to require a professional response. Simply, respond positively to each participant. Please apply the 'clean slate' concept during Character Circles and do not allow previous negative classroom behavior to exclude a student from fully participating.

NOTES TO THE GUIDE:

1. Some of the longer activities may be completed outside of the Character Circle session.
2. Participants who appear to not be affected may be affected the most. Try not to make assumptions or pass judgment. Be neutral and supportive.
3. Teachers who are guides are encouraged to not mix the two positions. Whereas a teacher is in charge of the classroom and may make certain comments, the guide is a participant and makes only supportive and positive comments to other participants.
4. Character Circle is a safe place for participants to express. Information shared in the Character Circle should not be held against participants in a separate setting.
5. Positive results will be achieved in any Character Circle where participants are comfortable and relaxed. Character Circle a non-threatening environment.
6. Be open-minded and show respect for all cultures.
7. You want the students to grasp the concept. Their responses will let you know if the message was clear.

QUESTIONS:

1. **Why do participants look into the mirror while sharing?** To encourage self-acceptance, boost self-esteem, and become more comfortable with themselves. You may notice the students are uncomfortable looking at themselves in the mirror initially, but quite comfortable by the middle of the Character Circle guidebook. Many participants are uncomfortable with who they are as individuals. Character Circles teach participants to become their own best friend; able to look into their own eyes will help the process.

2. **Why should the teacher act only as a guide while in the Character Circle?** The whole concept of the Character Circle is to help students feel safe to the point that they are willing to take down their security walls and begin to learn. If students feel pressured from a teacher in the Character Circle, they will not lower their barriers, which would defeat the purpose of the Character Circle.

CHARACTER CIRCLE OPTIONS AND IDEAS:

- Invite speakers with special needs and handicaps to share how they cope with being unique.
- Spread a beautiful piece of material on the classroom floor and have students sit around the edges.
- Limit student responses to 2 to 3 volunteers, according to the allotted time. Some students tend to deviate away from the topic. For example, they may begin to tell a story about their pet or another irrelevant topic. Promptly redirect the conversation, "Thank you for sharing Hanna, I can understand why you care for your pet."

Table of Contents

Lesson 1: Introduction

3 Target Components of Change:

⇒ **DISCOVERING SELF-EFFICACY**

⇒ **BUILDING ACADEMIC COMPETENCE**

⇒ **EMPOWERING THE LEARNER**

<u>CHANGING THE WAY YOU THINK</u>

Many students are unaware that the way they think affects how they learn. They have not learned the secret that succeeding and getting all A's can happen simply by changing the way you think. The first step is believing you can succeed at what you try. This is called **self-efficacy**. Changing the way you think will build your **self-efficacy**. You will begin to achieve and succeed at anything you practice. More students would succeed if they knew how to apply the principles you will learn in the *What You Say Is What You Are,* Activity Guide.

LET'S BEGIN OUR JOURNEY TO SUCCESS!

A Note From the Author:

Dear Reader:

When was the last time you said something nice to someone else?

____

When was the last time you said something nice to yourself?

____

This is your  heart.

This is your  mouth.

This is your 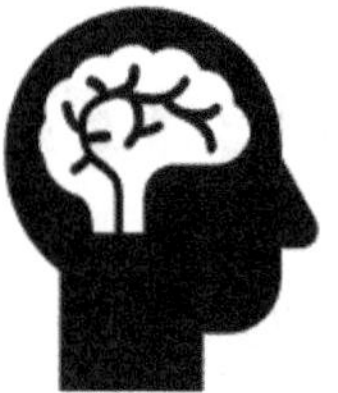 brain.

They are a very special team, communicating with each other every moment, even in your sleep.

Your mouth speaks whatever your heart believes. Your heart and brain believe whatever your mouth speaks.

Here's how they work: Your heart believes something (i.e., I'm cute.). The message travels on a field trip to your mouth. Your mouth opens, and you declare, "I am so hot!" And your brain soaks it all up like a sponge. This process determines your actions and affects your learning.

As an author, I could have written a book about anything at all, but I chose to write to help make children aware of the power of self-talk and how they can use it to build their self-efficacy as they strive to become their personal best.

In this guide, I want to bring you face to face with how your thoughts, beliefs, and actions affect your academic achievement.

Are you up for the challenge? _______

LET'S GO!

THUMBS UP! is our universal signal. 

It means we are being the best we can be at this moment.

You are about to begin your journey toward academic success. You will need to bring along rational thoughts and beliefs, a little **self-efficacy**, as well as a positive attitude and mindset.

Repeat after me: I can; I will; I believe; I am!

Lesson 2: Nametags

Question: What if I held out these two nametags and told you to choose one to wear around your neck? You have a choice to pick either one you want.

Which nametag would you pick?

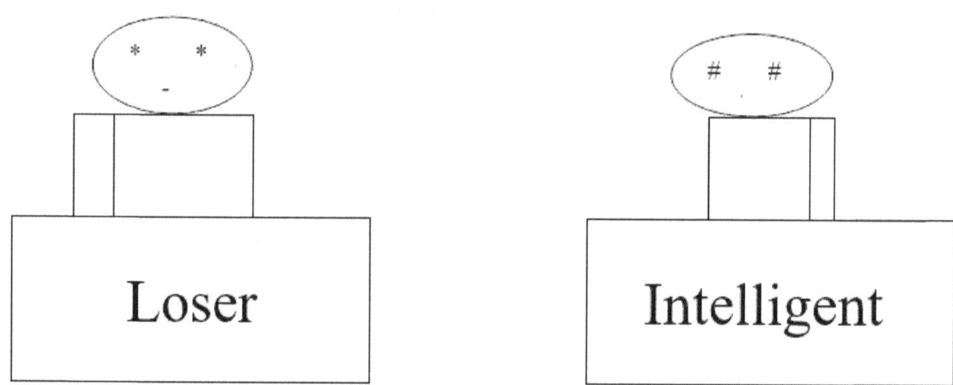

Sadly, some kids would pick the one that says, *Loser*.

Have you ever wondered . . .

- Why people get so upset when someone else calls them stupid but never get mad when they call themselves stupid?

- Why we want to fight others when they call us dumb when we say the very same thing to ourselves?

This thought leads me to another question: Whenever we call ourselves mean names, should we fight ourselves? Calling ourselves mean names is one of the silliest things we could ever do. It's even more ridiculous than fighting ourselves.

Why do some kids walk around day after day with a mean nametag around their neck and then have the nerve to get angry when someone calls out the name on their tag?

If you don't like your nametag, then it's time to stop wearing it. TAKE IT OFF NOW! And put on a new nametag.

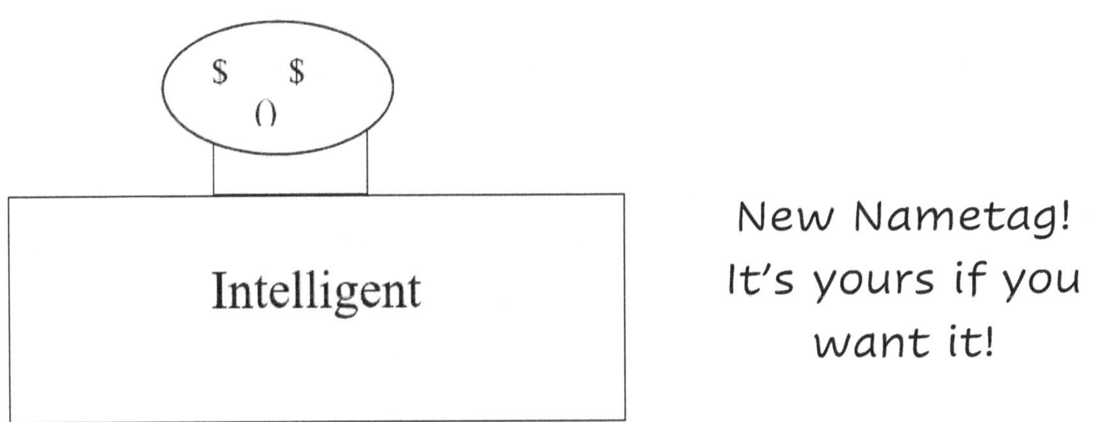

Guess What:

Your brain controls all of your thoughts and emotions. The more times you tell yourself you are not smart, the more you will believe it. When your brain believes it is not smart, it will make you act as though you are not smart. The messages sent from your brain control your reactions. Being smart is a goal that can be achieved through practice and studying.

Lesson 3: Self-Efficacy

⚡ News Flash:

> If you get D's and F's, it may be because
> you don't believe you can get A's and B's.

Messages are always traveling to and from our brains even when we are unaware of it. It happens automatically. Students who believe they are smart send positive messages to their brains, resulting in intelligent reactions. Being smart means studying, practicing, doing your best, and embracing **self-efficacy**.

The human brain is a special computer. Whatever we put into our brains is what we will get out. You can program your computer to do anything at all. It's so simple! Students who get A's and B's usually work very hard to get them. These students also have a strong belief that they can achieve success at any skill they practice. This action is an example of **self-efficacy**.

Let me tell you a little about the story book, 'What You Say Is What You Are.' It's a story about a regular kid just like you. His name is Andy. Andy is a really cool kid. He's the kind of friend we all like to have because he likes to give away stuff. For example, he'll give you his old PS5 or Nintendo game system if he gets a new one. And he always brings lots of candy to give away at school.

Here's another example of how cool Andy is:

It's lunchtime in the cafeteria. You open your lunch box only to find another asparagus, spinach, and artichoke sandwich.

Let's just say it's not your favorite.

Then Andy saves the day when he pulls out an extra scrumptious lunch pack and gives it to you.

Check all the statements you agree with:

_______   Andy is a cool kid.

_______   Andy is a good friend.

So, you would predict Andy is also nice to himself since he is nice to everyone else, right? That would make sense.

What I mean is, if I knew you to be a nice friend to others, I would not imagine that you change personalities once you get home after school and start fights with yourself.

I would not visualize you passing by the mirror in your house and speaking to your reflection, saying negative things like:

"What are you looking at?"
"You want some of this?"
"You want a piece of me?"

Let's see what happens when Andy gets home each day:

Mom: "Hi Andy, how was school today?"

Andy: "Same ole' thing."

Mom: "And how was your test?"

Andy: "Oh, I bombed it as usual. You know I'm not that smart."

Mom: "Andy, why are you so hard on yourself?"

Andy: "Because I'm worthless, not quite good at anything. For example, our whole class had to race today in PE, and guess who came in last? Even the girls beat me. I'm the slowest kid on the planet. A turtle could challenge me and win! Oh, and on my way home from school, I tripped over my own shadow. Where did you get such a clumsy kid like me?"

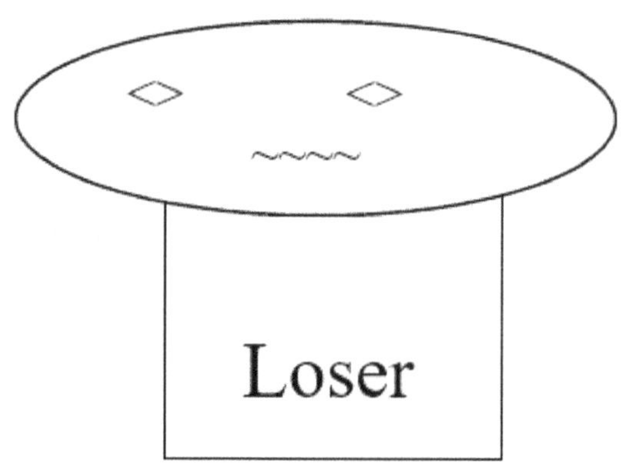

I don't do anything right.
Just call me, 'Loser!'

"My teacher wants me to play baseball, but I told her no way. I'm not good at baseball. I'm not good at any sports. I'm not good at anything. I'm just a lousy ole' kid."

Check all the statements you agree with now:

________   Andy is a cool kid.

________   Andy is a good friend.

________   Andy is a good friend to himself.

Lesson 4: Self-Esteem

I agree with you. Andy is a terrible friend to himself. **But why?** Why would anyone treat everyone else kindly but say mean and hurtful things to themself?

"Ohhh, I know! I'll tell you why."

Inside all of us is something called **self-esteem**. It's how a person feels about themself. **Self-esteem** can be positive (which is good) or negative (not so good).

**But what determines if your self-esteem
is positive or negative?**

There are two voices inside of you that I have given names. Goodina and Evelin. These voices are also called **self-talk**, which is the way you talk to yourself in your mind.

When Goodina gets into your **self-esteem**, your **self-talk** is good. It convinces your heart you are special and sends positive messages to your heart, mouth, and brain.

These are the students who walk around saying things like:
"I just know I can win."
"I'm the most handsome person in the world."
Or, "I'm so smart."

But when Evelin gets into your **self-talk**, it convinces your heart you are *not* special and sends mean, cruel messages to your heart, mouth, and brain. These are the students who walk around saying things like:
"I could never be that pretty."
"I'll never make the honor roll."
"Nobody likes me."
Or, "I'm sure I failed the test again."

Which of these personalities is most like you?

Check all that are true:

________ Do you listen to the voice of Goodina and have a positive self-esteem? OR . . .

________ Are you more like Andy? Do you listen to the voice of Evelin and have a negative self-esteem?

________ Do you say mean things to yourself?

It may have been funny earlier when I asked if we should fight ourselves whenever we call ourselves mean names, but that is exactly what people with low self-esteem do. They beat themselves up with their own words.

Do you feel sorry for Andy right now?

Circle Your Response: Yes   No

Well, there is good news for Andy. He has a special friend who helps him learn a very special lesson. It's his pet parrot, Fred. But Fred cannot fly out of the story to help you. You have to allow Goodina, your positive self-talk, to lead you to loving yourself and feeling good about who you are. Andy became a better friend to himself in the conclusion.

THUMBS UP! 

If you are like Andy was at the beginning of the story, you can change. You can have positive **self-esteem** by saying, "NO!"

Say, "**NO!**" to every voice that tells you that you can't.

Say, "**NO!**" to anyone who tells you that you cannot succeed.

Say, "**NO!**" to irrational thoughts and beliefs.

Say, "**NO!**"

Just say, "**NO!**"

Remember:
What you say is what you are.
You believe, and you'll go far.
If in your heart you do believe.
Then I know you will achieve.

THUMBS UP! 

Lesson 5: Seeds

Question and answers:

1. **How do people get negative self-esteem?**
   Self-Esteem starts out as a little seed, like a pea. It begins to grow
   when we feel good or bad about ourselves.

Self Esteem Seed 

But it depends on what type of *food* is being fed to the seed. For
example, natural plants grow when they receive water and sunlight.

But if a plant is given poisonous chemicals, such as bleach, then the
plant will die.

In the same way, self-esteem grows when you and the people around
you give you lots of love.

If you have low self-esteem, it may not be all your fault.

A lot of it has to do with how others have treated you since you were born. Whether you were held a lot as a baby or just left alone in a crib. Whether you were dressed up fancy as a baby boy or girl and got a lot of presents and attention. Or ignored as a baby because you had many other siblings to share the attention with. Whether people walked by and said, "What an adorable, cute baby!" Or instead, just stared at you. These types of treatment affect us all in different ways.

It also has to do with your life now: Whether someone is around to talk with you and hold you, rather than someone who pushes you away and says that you are a pest. It depends on whether someone is home to greet you after school and help you with homework. Or whether you have someone in your life who seems to care if you had a terrible day or have enough food to eat.

If you have been in some of these terrible situations, you may feel like you have an excuse to engage in irrational thinking, but you don't. Remember that you are responsible for your emotions.

Lesson 6: Choices

Life is all about choices.

People make choices every day. Choosing positive self-talk is one way of taking responsibility for your emotions.

So even if you say, "No one loves you", remember you must love yourself. And if no one believes in you, you must believe in yourself.

No one controls you with a remote. You are not a robot.

You can choose to be happy no matter what your life is like.

Just call me a star!

Sure, I've got faults just like everyone else. Some of my days are dumpy, but some are also great. Sometimes the people I love forget to tell me or show me any love at all. But I remember that they are not perfect. So, I can choose to be angry, blame them, and harbor hate in my heart for them, or I can say to myself, "I love you and I believe in you. You are a winner." I can even give myself a hug every once in a while.

This is called, 'looking on the bright side.'

If you traveled the world, you would see that your life isn't so bad after all.

Some kids have no parents or home.

When you remember the bad things in your life, remind yourself of the good things.

What you say is what you are!

If you say that you are a winner,
then that's exactly what you are, my friend.

Hello winner!

What you say is what you are.

You believe, and you'll go far.

If in your heart you do believe,

then I know you will achieve.

I can; I will; I believe; I am!

I believe it in my heart.

I can see it in my dreams.

It's imprinted in my mind.

I will succeed!

THUMBS UP!

Lesson 7: Personality Check

Understanding your personality will help you to make wise academic choices.

Personality Check

<u>Objective</u>: Students will conduct a self-evaluation and identify with one of two personality disposition (positive or negative).

<u>Aim</u>: Students will realize that how they view themselves as individuals can affect their learning.

<u>Lesson</u>: *What is self-esteem?* It's the way a person feels about themself.

Some people love the way they look. They believe they are the most special people in the world. They smile all the time because they know their smiles are beautiful. These people are confident and optimistic. They have self-efficacy and believe they can succeed at anything they try. They never give up because they believe in themselves.

Are you one of these positive people? (Circle One)

Yes   Sometimes   Not Really

There are also people who hate the way they look. They rarely smile because they believe they are not special. These people often say mean things to themselves. For example, they may say, "I am so fat!" or "I hate my lips!" or "I'm so stupid!" or "I'm the biggest loser!" They have low self-efficacy and believe they will fail at most things they try.

Are you one of these negative people? (Circle One)

Yes   Sometimes   Not Really

Remember: *If you don't like yourself very much, then you may have the wrong attitude towards learning. The second personality disposition negatively affects how you learn. No matter which personality you have, you should know you are unique and special to this world. You should know you are a piece of a big puzzle, and the world would be incomplete without you.*

Positive Affirmation:

In a mirror, say:
I am special,
just the way I am.

THUMBS UP! 

Lesson 8:
Rational vs. Irrational Thinking
Part 1

**The way you feel about yourself
has a lot to do with the way you think.**

Let's Investigate:

<u>Objective</u>: Students will learn how to recognize and make a distinction between rational and irrational thoughts and beliefs.

<u>Aim</u>: Students understand that they don't have to embrace a thought just because it runs through their minds. Students learn to identify, embrace, and engage in rational thinking; and to ignore irrational thoughts and beliefs, which hinder learning.

<u>Lesson</u>: Irrational Thinking: Thinking in a way that is **not** sensible or fair. Irrational thinking puts pressure on oneself and leads to irrational beliefs. Irrational thinking is the culprit for why some students fail or refuse even to try.

THUMBS UP! 

Irrational thinking affects your learning because when you think you are not smart, you may not put much effort into what you are trying to learn.

An Example of Irrational Thinking:

Situation: Your teacher introduces a new math problem.

Irrational Thinking: Great, a new math problem, and I haven't even learned the last one. I'm the dumbest one in the class. I'm sure I won't get this problem either.

Irrational Belief: I'm just not good at math. I fail even when I try. I always get bad grades in math.

Now that's not entirely true or fair, is it? Giving up on a skill before even trying it is *absolutely* not fair. Giving up after only one, two, or a few tries isn't fair either. Giving yourself a fair chance to succeed means getting enough practice.

Example of Rational Thinking:

Think about skills you do well, like riding a bike or tying a pair of shoelaces. Write two skills you do well on the lines below.

1. _______________________________
2. _______________________________

You are good at these skills only because you've had enough practice. ***Do you remember the first time you tried these skills?*** You probably were not as good at them then as you are now, and you owe it all to practice. This example of *your* learning proves you are intelligent and have the ability to learn new skills.

Learning in school works the same way. A particular lesson may seem difficult initially, but you become good at it with enough practice and interest. It eventually seems easier because learning becomes more manageable with practice.

The next time you are confronted with a new challenge and irrational thoughts come to your mind, remember that you have a choice:

A. Embrace the irrational thoughts and feel sorry for yourself.
B. Replace the irrational thoughts with rational thoughts and feel like a champion.

<u>**Remember:**</u> You can identify irrational thoughts when you begin to feel helplessness and self-pity. You do not have to believe a thought just because it comes to your mind. Ignore irrational thoughts and replace them quickly with rational ones.

Positive Affirmation:

In a mirror, say: Irrational thinking is not for me. I choose to think rationally. I believe I can succeed. I have many skills.

THUMBS UP! 

Lesson 9:
Rational vs. Irrational Thinking
Part 2

Objective: Students will learn that irrational thinking may affect their academic passion by causing them to feel unimportant and unworthy.

Aim: Students come to appreciate who they are as individuals and embrace the concept that their uniqueness makes them special and worthy. Students ignore thoughts that attack their academic focus. Students identify their strengths and build on them.

Lesson: Rational Thinking: thinking in a way that is **sensible, reasonable, and fair**. Rational thinking builds self-efficacy and leads to success.

Another Example of Irrational Thinking:

Situation: You did not get picked for a team at recess.

Irrational Thinking: More kids would like me and want me on their team if I was a faster runner.

Irrational Belief: I'm not popular, and nobody likes me because I'm slow.

Now that's not entirely true, is it? Even if you do run slowly, there are still many people who like you just the way you are, and how fast you run has nothing to do with the reasons why they like you. But the important thing is what *you* say. ***Do you like yourself just the way you are?***

Example of Rational Thinking:

When you embrace the irrational thoughts about not being liked because you run slowly, you are sending your brain a message that you are unimportant and unworthy.

These thoughts trigger unfavorable emotions, which can ruin your entire day and cause you to be unable to focus on learning once you return to class. Send a positive rational message by saying:

> "The way I run is one of the unique
> qualities that make me who I am.
> The way I run has nothing
> to do with this situation."

Remember: It is normal to have irrational thoughts but replacing them quickly with rational reasonable thoughts will allow you to gain the most from your academic experiences.

Positive Affirmation:

In a mirror, say:
I love being who I am.
I have many strengths.
I am unique, special, and
worthy of the best.

THUMBS UP! 

Lesson 10:
Rational vs. Irrational Thinking
Part 3

ACTIVITY:

The situations in the table below sometimes cause people to engage in irrational thinking. Think about some of the things that cause you to feel upset or embarrassed.

Now, put a check mark √ next to the situations below that cause you to feel upset or embarrassed:

___ failing a test

___ not being invited to a birthday party

___ making a mistake in class

___ lying to your parents

___ saying a bad comment to a friend

___ getting the star role in a play

___ when someone forgets to thank you for something

___ being picked last at recess

___ being corrected by a teacher

___ getting straight A's on your report card

___ when your best friend gets close to another friend

ACTIVITY:

Write at least three of the situations you put a check mark by on a sheet of paper. Now, explain how you feel after each of these incidents happen and describe the thoughts that pass through your mind.

FACT:

Everyone has irrational thoughts sometimes, and that's normal. However, too much irrational thinking can put a great deal of pressure on you and cause you to feel sad most of the time.

Lesson 11:
Rational vs. Irrational Thinking
Part 4

Irrational Thinking is especially bad because it discourages self-acceptance. It makes you feel like you are not good enough. You will be the best that you can be when you learn to love yourself just the way you are and begin to build on your personal strengths.

- What is your favorite subject? _______________________________
- What part of this subject can you do well? _______________________

____

This subject is one of your strengths!

Always Remember:

✓ Your uniqueness is the very thing that makes you special.
✓ Irrational beliefs cause students to believe being **different** is a bad thing.

If you have ever put a puzzle together, you may have noticed that each piece is different. Yet, all the pieces are equally important since the puzzle is incomplete unless every piece is included. If you place the wrong piece in a certain spot, it will not fit.

In the same way, you are an important piece in the puzzle of this world. Without you, the world would be incomplete. If you were just like someone else, there would be no need for you in the puzzle since two similar pieces cannot fit in the same spot. So, now you can see why **being different is actually kind of cool.** No one can take your place in the puzzle because you are the only one that will fit just right.

Positive Affirmation:

In a mirror, say:
I will think rationally
and not put unfair pressure
on myself.
I love being different,
unique, and special.
It makes me who I am.
I am intelligent!

THUMBS UP! 

Lesson 12:
Emotions, Emotions, Emotions
Part 1

Emotions affect your learning. Whereas one emotion may cause you to feel motivated to work harder, another may cause you to feel helpless and like giving up. Emotions can create a roller coaster effect creating an inconsistency in your academic achievement.

Every Person Has Emotions:

Objective: The students identify their emotions and understand emotions can be controlled.

Aim: The students take responsibility for making wise choices when dealing with their emotions.

Lesson: Emotions are feelings. For example, *happy, sad, bored, excited, or indifferent.*

It's normal to have several different emotions throughout the day. However, each person must take responsibility for their own emotions and not blame others for how they feel. It's true that people can say or do things that trigger a particular emotion, but how you react to their actions is something you must take responsibility for.

THUMBS UP! 

Here's how emotions affect self-efficacy:

Let's say Andy gets upset at another student in his class. Andy decides to shut down and stop listening to the teacher's test review lesson because the other student made him mad. Andy may not realize it, but he is actually punishing himself and not the other student who made him upset. Andy may end up failing the test since he did not hear what the teacher had to say. If Andy does fail the test, who should he blame?

ACTIVITY:

Read each question and circle A or B.

1. Who do you blame when you are sad?

A. I blame myself.   **B.** I blame the person who made me sad.

2. Who do you blame when you are angry?

A. I blame myself.   **B.** I blame the person who made me angry.

Lesson 13:
Emotions, Emotions, Emotions
Part 2

When you blame others for your emotions, you are not taking responsibility for your actions.

Think about it: Blaming others for your reactions is like saying other people control you like a remote controls a robot. Deciding to stop listening to his teacher was Andy's decision. Even though the other student's action may have caused Andy to feel upset, Andy is responsible for making the best decision about how to react to the way he feels. The other student did not punch a code into a remote that caused Andy to react the way he did. Therefore, if Andy fails the test, he has to blame himself since he handled his emotion the wrong way.

Listen friend, it's okay to feel angry when your best friend forgets to save a seat for you at lunch, but it's not okay or fair to blame your best friend for how *you* feel and how *you* choose to react.

If you say that another student caused you to strike him, you are actually saying that the student you hit is in control of your actions.

Positive Affirmation:

In a mirror, say:
I will take responsibility
for my emotions and
not allow others to
control my reactions.

Lesson 14:
Emotions, Emotions, Emotions
Part 3

ACTIVITY: Find the words in the puzzle.

My Emotions and Feelings are Important.

```
D S D W Z I F F A E K N E D D
E D U A T C H N C D O L U E E
N E Y O S N G W E D B Q C I S
E V W Y I R E X Q A K O G F S
T E A X Y C E R R D N N J S A
H I D F V L I E E F E E H I R
G L F E P B S P I F A T U T R
I E J R T I H D S L F C R A A
R R E F M S E R O U N I T S B
F P G H D N U U V E S B D R M
L B M M T A S G D E R O B N E
H A P P Y F M P S M U M K Q I
L U F E T A R G A I Y V A A S
D H W Q N D L P Q Z D T O H R
C L I W R H A G N A H G K A O
```

ANGRY	GRATEFUL	MISERABLE
BORED	HAPPY	RELIEVED
CONFIDENT	HURT	PERPLEXED
DISGUSTED	INDIFFERENT	SATISFIED
EMBARRASSED	JEALOUS	SAD
FRIGHTENED	MAD	

Lesson 15:
I'm in Charge of My Emotions
Part 1

Taking control of your emotions will enable you to get the most out of your learning experiences.

Objective: The students will learn to embrace positive emotions and build self-efficacy.

Aim: The students construct positive affirmations, which they will use to gain control of their emotions and thoughts to the benefit of their academic achievements.

Always Remember:
✓ Negative emotions should not be entertained.
✓ Try to replace emotions like anger quickly.

Here's how you can change an emotion like anger:

Practice Example: In a situation where Andy's best friend forgets to save him a seat in the cafeteria, it's easy for Andy to become angry. So naturally, negative thoughts about his best friend will begin to come into Andy's mind. But rather than entertaining the negative thoughts and allowing them to run through his mind all day long, Andy can make a decision to react positively to the situation. **How should Andy react?**

Remember: Choosing a negative reaction may cause Andy to be upset for the rest of the day and not perform at his best when he returns to his classroom.

ACTIVITY:
Select the best reaction for Andy.

A. Andy should take a deep breath and admit to himself that he feels jealous and angry. Then he should tell himself that sometimes it's okay for his best friend to sit with his other friends if that makes him happy. Finally, Andy should remind himself of all the good things he likes about his best friend since doing so will stop the negative thoughts in his mind.

B. Andy should walk up to his best friend and tell him that they are no longer friends. Then Andy should write an angry letter blaming his best friend for making him end the friendship. Andy should make sure that his ex-best friend knows this is all his fault.

One secret to taking control of your emotions is admitting how you feel. Your emotions are important, and you should never feel ashamed about the way you feel.

Remember: We are in charge of our own emotions. Therefore, Andy can choose to be forgiving.

THUMBS UP! 

Lesson 16:
Speak to Your Emotions

Speak To Your Emotions; Watch Them Obey and Change!

Here are some examples of how to speak to your emotions.

Situation: Someone calls you a mean name at school.

Initial Emotion: You are angry.

Say: I am not the name that person called me. I know who I am.

New Emotion: I am confident.

Situation: You fall while running in the cafeteria and kids laugh.

Initial Emotion: You feel embarrassed.

Say: Sometimes it's funny when people fall, as long as they are not hurt. I am not hurt. I can laugh at myself too.

New Emotion: I feel silly.

Now you try it:

Situation: You have to read your book report before the entire school.

Initial Emotion: You feel ___________________________.

Say: ____

____

New Emotion: ___________________________________

So, you see it's that simple to control irrational thoughts and emotions by speaking a positive statement to yourself each time you have a negative thought.

Positive Affirmation:

In a mirror, say: I'm in charge of my emotions and I choose to be happy and positive.

Lesson 17:
Factors That Affect Your Learning

Objective: Students will examine various factors involved in their academic experiences.

Aim: Students realize emotions are natural and automatic yet can be displaced.

Lesson: People have many sides. Some days you may feel clumsy and drop everything you hold, trip over the chair's leg in the classroom, and spill juice on your favorite outfit.

But on another day, you make no mistakes at all. If all your days were free of mistakes, that would mean you are perfect and **no one is perfect!**

Andy experienced several different emotions during one day, from being excited about his friends to being frustrated about his mistakes. It's perfectly normal to have several different emotions even in one day.

ACTIVITY: Circle your response to each question.

1. How did Andy feel when he compared himself to the other children at the modeling agency?

   bored   jealous   excited   indifferent

2. Have you ever known someone who said they could not do something before even trying:

   YES or NO

3. Have you ever given up after trying or practicing something only once?

YES or NO

This is called **learned helplessness**. It's time to bury the words, 'I can't.' These words will cause you to miss out on some of the best things in life.

ACTIVITY:

Ask four people to please pick two emotions from the list below that they would feel if they were standing in the modeling agency from the story. Then write their responses on the lines below.

A. **Angry** because my parents don't believe that I'm beautiful enough to sign me up for modeling.
B. **Sympathetic** because those poor kids don't have a normal life.
C. **Confident** because I know I'm just as beautiful as the models.
D. **Jealous** because I wish I looked as beautiful as the models.
E. **Disappointed** because my parents sent me to regular school when I could be making millions of dollars as a model.
F. **Indifferent** because I don't care about being a model or looking like one.

Person 1: _________________________   _________________________

Person 2: _________________________   _________________________

Person 3: _________________________   _________________________

Person 4: _________________________   _________________________

You may notice the responses from persons 1 through 4 are different. That is because each person is unique and has different ways of dealing with situations. Not all emotions must be embraced and expressed. Sometimes emotions can be replaced by exchanging them with a more appropriate emotion. It's a conscious effort that can be learned.

If you have an emotion that causes you to feel like giving up, that emotion should be replaced. It is natural to feel like giving up sometimes, but do not express it by refusing to give your best attention to your academics. Allowing your emotions to interfere with your learning is a harmful mistake that will affect your success later in life.

Remember:
✓ Emotions are natural and normal.
✓ Negative emotions can be displaced, eliminated, and replaced by positive emotions.

Positive Affirmation:

In a mirror, say:
I will make good decisions about my emotions and embrace the ones that build my academic confidence.

THUMBS UP! 

Lesson 18:
The Brain Train

ACTIVITY:

Analyze each message in the cars below. Fill in the blanks by labeling the *Brain Train* cars: positive and rational thinking OR negative and irrational thinking.

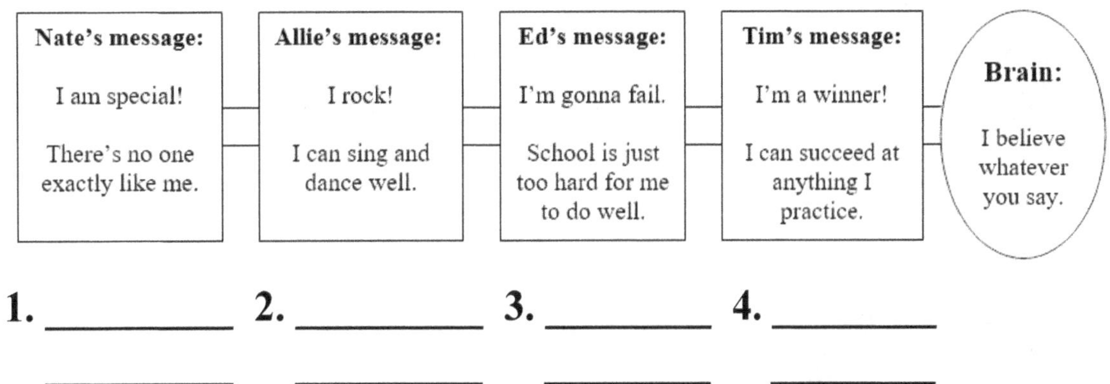

1. __________ 2. __________ 3. __________ 4. __________

__________ __________ __________ __________

The brain receives messages based on what you believe. Let's say that on Monday, your teacher announced there will be a math test on Friday. You will automatically have a positive or negative thought based on the way you feel about tests. This thought comes from your past experiences with tests.

Let's look at an example:

Belief: Tests are hard. I'm not good at math.

Negative Thought: I hate tests. I always fail.

Negative Statement: I'm just gonna get another 'F'.

Message to Brain: There is no hope of passing.

Brain's Reaction: Do not practice. Do not try.

Your Reaction: Watch TV and play video games all day.

Test Results: You get an 'F' because you programmed your brain to fail.

Look at the same situation with a different belief and attitude.

On Monday, your teacher announced there will be a math test on Friday.

Belief: Practice makes perfect.
Positive Thought: Maybe this time I can pass the test.
Positive Statement: I will practice harder this time.
Message to Brain: There is a chance of passing.
Brain's Reaction: Reminds you to study often.
Your Reaction: You take turns studying and playing.
Test Results: You pass because you programmed your brain to succeed.

Your brain can only put out what you put into it!

THUMBS UP! 

Lesson 19:
The Brain Train Summary

Let's Summarize

You have a choice of positive or negative self-esteem, rational or irrational thoughts and beliefs, and appropriate or inappropriate emotions:

Your reactions all depend on the messages you are sending to your brain.

ACTIVITY:

Put a check on the line next to the response that best fits your personality.

<u>Situation:</u> You are having a bad hair day.

_____ I'm as ugly as a raccoon.

_____ Oh no! I'm having a bad hair day, but it will be better tomorrow. Everybody has bad hair days sometimes.

<u>Situation:</u> You failed your spelling test.

_____ I deserve an 'F' because I'm stupid, and I always fail anyway.

_____ I really didn't study as hard as I could have.

The problem is *not* the situation; it's *your* attitude toward the situation. Some thoughts produce hurtful emotions. So, think positively!

ACTIVITY: Write a story about a time when you said something mean to yourself. Describe how you felt.

____

____

____

____

____

____

____

____

____

ACTIVITY Write a story about a time when you said something kind to yourself. Describe how you felt.

____

____

____

____

____

____

____

____

____

____

THUMBS UP! 

Lesson 20:
A Note From the Author

Dear reader,

Congratulations on your journey so far. At this point, you are aware of self-efficacy. You have begun to build your academic competence, and you are feeling empowered. By now, I hope you understand that people are not born smart or dumb, but rather that people become smarter by practicing skills.

By now, I hope you understand how the way you think affects your accomplishments. I have shown you how irrational thoughts and beliefs, as well as negative emotions and attitudes, hinder your success.

A wise man named Nelson Mandela once said that each human being possesses a certain level of greatness inside. Understanding how to apply self-efficacy to shape your destiny while you are young will help you to find your true purpose in life and develop your personal greatness as an adult.

So, I will say it again: The way you think affects how you learn. Change the way you think. When faced with any task, speak to your brain, heart, and emotions. Always believe that you will win and succeed at the things you practice. Tell your brain that you can do it! Let's continue our journey.

-Coach 

A True Story: The Double Dutch Klutz

Annie gets straight A's in school and always makes the honor roll. In math, she learns the concept on the 1st day. She is an academic star.

Lisa is the complete opposite of Annie. Lisa gets F's on just about every test and has never made the honor roll. It takes Lisa weeks to learn new math concepts. Lisa is a sweet girl, though not quite an academic star.

Joshua is right between the two girls. He makes mostly C's and some B's, and he has made the honor roll in the past.

One day the teacher announced to the students, "All kids can learn. Everyone in this classroom and around the world can succeed at any skill that they program their brains to master."

Some of the students began to discuss the teacher's comments amongst themselves. "Are you saying that we all have the same brain?" one student asked. "Some kids are just smarter than others and get A's because they are just smarter," another student said.

Then the teacher spoke, "I am saying that all students have the same ability to teach their brain a new skill."

"I don't know," said Lisa. "I don't think that I can catch on to a new skill as fast as Annie. She's just smarter."

"But what makes Annie smarter, and why does she get all A's?" asked the teacher.

The class was silent for a time, then Joshua replied, "because she got a better brain, that's why." The students chuckled.

After thinking for a while, the teacher said, "I have a little challenge for this class. I will prove to all of you that there is one word that identifies the reason why some students succeed while others fail.

Beginning Monday, our class will Double Dutch jump rope every day for fifteen minutes. All students are welcome to join in, but no one will be forced to participate. You will jump when you want and sit out when you need to."

"What's the one word?" Joshua asked.

"Oh, it's PRACTICE," the teacher said proudly. Here is the challenge for you: Any student who practices Double Dutch for fifteen minutes each day for ten weeks will master the skill. In addition to practicing, each student must only say positive self-statements like, "I will learn."

Joshua was quite tickled, and he laughed. "Boys can't jump rope," he declared.

"Really?" the teacher perplexed.

As planned, Double Dutch practices began. Every student tried the skill the first few days. Some grew bored or just gave up and decided to quit saying phrases like, "I knew I wouldn't get it" and, "it's too hard." More than half the class continued jumping for at least two weeks but skipped days here and there. Some days they believed they could do it, and the next day they would give up. Annie, Lisa, and Joshua never missed one day. They practiced and made positive self-statements like, "I know I can do it" and "I'm a Double Dutch star."

By the end of the third week, Lisa had mastered the skill of Double Dutch. Joshua also 'got the hang' of Double Dutch the following Monday. The teacher was happy for the students and proud that her challenge was a success.

As the fifth week came to an end, the teacher began to grow anxious because, for some strange reason, Annie had not mastered the skill. In fact, it appeared that she would never get it. Annie remained focused. She kept saying positive statements to herself and practiced every single day. *So, what was the problem?*

The teacher forgot about the challenge and began to worry about how Annie's confidence would be affected if she failed at this skill. "What if she doesn't learn to Double Dutch; will she stop believing that she can do anything she puts her mind to?" The teacher pondered this in her heart for weeks.

Lisa and Joshua continued to practice every day and got better. They cheered for Annie and encouraged her not to give up, and she didn't. Annie tripped, fell, and scratched her knees all throughout the seventh week. She got tangled in the ropes in the eighth week and got hit in the face by the ropes towards the end of the ninth week.

On Monday of the tenth week, the teacher said to Annie, "I believe in you even if you do not conquer Double Dutch this week. I'm sure you will get it as long as you continue practicing."

On Tuesday, Annie said to the teacher, "I'm gonna take a break from Double Dutch." The teacher looked Annie in the eyes and said, "You are so close. I entered this entire team in the school's talent show to share our challenge with the entire school, and I believe you will be in this show."

Annie played on the playground on Tuesday but was back to jumping on Wednesday. "She did it!" Lisa and Joshua screamed loud enough to wake the dead, "She did it!" The teacher ran over to the Double Dutch ropes, and sure enough, Annie made three successful jumps before falling.

The teacher's faith was renewed, and she allowed the students to practice for fifteen extra minutes for the next three days. By Thursday, Annie had mastered the skill, though it was painful just to watch her jump. Annie lifted her legs so high as she jumped and stumbled around in the ropes as if she was about to fall. But she didn't fall that day, and she didn't fall in the talent show.

Annie's enthusiasm made her exciting to watch. The audience noticed that Annie's jumping was unusual, but they just believed it was her style. Joshua received special applause for being the only boy in the show. One man shouted from the audience, "You go, boy!" Who said boys can't jump rope?

Lisa, well, Lisa was a natural. She jumped with ease and learned many tricks. Each of the students learned to turn the ropes as well as how to jump in while the ropes were in motion.

This challenge caught the attention of the entire school. More students from other classrooms came out each day during practice to watch the challenge.

So what if Annie's jump looked funny? All that mattered was that she got it. The teacher proved to the class that any skill could be learned if it is practiced enough. Lisa learned an important lesson. Her brain was just as good as Annie's, after all. Lisa began to study more often at home and practiced new math skills every day. Her grades began to get better. Joshua became a straight 'A' student in math.

Each time the students made positive statements; they were sending positive messages to their brains. This is how the brain is programmed. Remember that the teacher challenged her entire class of twenty-four students, but only three of them met the challenge.

Guess what happened to the students that gave up and said that Double Dutch was too hard and that they would not get it. They didn't get it! Not because it was too hard, but because they didn't practice. They programmed their brains to fail and missed out on learning a really tough but *really* cool skill for many kids.

ACTIVITY:

Write your response to each question.

1. Can you Double Dutch?

   ____

2. Would you succeed at the challenge like Annie, Lisa, and Joshua?

   ____

3. Would you have given up like most of the students did?

   ____

4. What if Annie did not succeed at the challenge until the 13th week? Would that mean that she failed?

   ____

Explain your answer:

____

____

____

5. Write about a challenge you succeeded at because you practiced and stuck with it.

____

____

____

____

____

____

____

____

Lesson 21:
Are You Programmed to Fail or Succeed?

If you knew you could program your brain to succeed, would you do it?

There are three kinds of programmers.

- I.   Adults – parents, teachers, in-laws, neighbors, etc.
- II.   Peers – siblings, friends, cousins, etc.
- III.   Self - you

People can be mean sometimes and say things that really hurt. Remember that you are not what others say you are. You are what **YOU** say you are.

YOU are the most important programmer. Your brain listens to the messages sent from your heart. Even though other programmers have some influence in shaping your beliefs, always remember to believe that you are special. If someone calls you ugly, that does not make it true. That is their opinion. What matters is what *you* say. You should look in the mirror and say, "I am beautiful and unique. I don't look like anyone else. I have my own look. I am different, and that makes me special."

Who is the most important programmer in your life? Who is the person who controls the way you feel about yourself? Is it your parents, friends, teachers, yourself, or someone else? Be honest. Write your response on the line. Explain.

____

____

____

____

Throughout the story in the Mentor Text, Andy recited negative statements to himself. Imagine how Andy would react and what he might have said if the following situations happened to him at a time *before* he learned to be positive. On the second line, write what Andy could say instead to help build his self-efficacy.

Incident: Falling off his bike
Andy might say:____
Andy could say: ____

Incident: Not being picked for the team
Andy might say:____
Andy could say: ____

Incident: Getting a bad test grade
Andy might say:____
Andy could say: ____

Incident: Missing the last basket and losing the game
Andy might say:____
Andy could say: ____

Incident: Not getting invited to the 'cool' kids' party
Andy might say:____
Andy could say: ____

Lesson 22:
Practicing Programming Activity 1
ACTIVITY:

Pretend that these situations happened to you. Practice programming your brain to think rationally and positively by writing your positive response for each incident (see examples on page 38).

Incident: Falling off your bike in front of your peers

Belief: _______________________________________

Positive Thought: _______________________________________

Positive Statement: _______________________________________

Message to Brain: _______________________________________

Brain's Reaction: _______________________________________

Your Reaction: _______________________________________

Outcome: _______________________________________

1. What emotions would you feel as a result of this incident?

   _______________ _______________ _______________

   (Remember it's okay to have more than one emotion at a time.)

2. Who would you blame for your emotions?

   ____

3. Describe one irrational thought that may cross your mind.

   ____

4. Explain how self-efficacy may help you to gain control of this emotion. _______________________________________

   ____

Lesson 23:
Practicing Programming Activity 2

ACTIVITY:

Pretend that these situations happened to you. Practice programming your brain to think rationally and positively by writing your positive response for each incident (see examples on page 38).

Incident: You were not picked for the team with the 'cool' kids

Belief: _______________________________

Positive Thought: _______________________________

Positive Statement: _______________________________

Message to Brain: _______________________________

Brain's Reaction: _______________________________

Your Reaction: _______________________________

Outcome: _______________________________

1. What emotions would you feel as a result of this incident?

___________________ ___________________ ___________________

   (Remember it's okay to have more than one emotion at a time.)

2. Who would you blame for your emotions?

____

3. Describe one irrational thought that may cross your mind.

____

4. Explain how self-efficacy may help you to gain control of this emotion._______________________________

____

Practicing Programming Activity 3

ACTIVITY:

Pretend that these situations happened to you. Practice programming your brain to think rationally and positively by writing your positive response for each incident (see examples on page 38).

Incident: You earned a bad test grade

Belief: ____
Positive Thought: _______________________________________
Positive Statement: _____________________________________
Message to Brain: _______________________________________
Brain's Reaction: _______________________________________
Your Reaction: ____
Outcome: ____

1. What emotions would you feel as a result of this incident?

   ___________________ ___________________ ___________________

   (Remember it's okay to have more than one emotion at a time.)

2. Who would you blame for your emotions?

____

3. Describe one irrational thought that may cross your mind.

____

4. Explain how self-efficacy may help you to gain control of this emotion.____

____

Lesson 24:
Practicing Programming Activity 4

ACTIVITY:

Pretend that these situations happened to you. Practice programming your brain to think rationally and positively by writing your positive response for each incident (see examples on page 38).

Incident: You missed the last basket and lost the game

Belief: _______________________________

Positive Thought: _______________________________

Positive Statement: _______________________________

Message to Brain: _______________________________

Brain's Reaction: _______________________________

Your Reaction: _______________________________

Outcome: _______________________________

1. What emotions would you feel as a result of this incident?

_______________ _______________ _______________

   (Remember it's okay to have more than one emotion at a time.)

2. Who would you blame for your emotions?

____

3. Describe one irrational thought that may cross your mind.

____

4. Explain how self-efficacy may help you to gain control of this emotion._______________________________

____

Practicing Programming Activity 5

ACTIVITY:

Pretend that these situations happened to you. Practice programming your brain to think rationally and positively by writing your positive response for each incident (see examples on page 38).

Incident: You were not invited to the 'cool' kids' party

Belief: ________________________________

Positive Thought: ________________________________

Positive Statement: ________________________________

Message to Brain: ________________________________

Brain's Reaction: ________________________________

Your Reaction: ________________________________

Outcome: ________________________________

1. What emotions would you feel as a result of this incident?

____________ ____________ ____________

   (Remember it's okay to have more than one emotion at a time.)

2. Who would you blame for your emotions?

____

3. Describe one irrational thought that may cross your mind.

____

4. Explain how self-efficacy may help you to gain control of this emotion.________________________________

____

Lesson 25: Be Realistic

No one is great at everything. We all have both weak and strong points. This means that you may be a great tennis player but not such an excellent football player.

You may be better at tennis because you have an interest in that sport and have spent endless hours practicing your skills. Football, on the other hand, may not appeal to you at all. You have not practiced it because you have no interest in it. Therefore, when you are challenged at football, you may lose the match.

That does not make you a loser. It doesn't mean that you should begin practicing every day for a rematch unless you really want to. It's okay not to have an interest in football.

School and academics are a different story. Students tend to get better grades in the subjects they actually enjoy. Every student does not prefer the same subjects. Some may favor Reading and Spelling, but Math and Science may not appeal to them. However, unlike sports, education is vital to success in life. What you have to do, is redirect your feelings by making positive statements. For example, you can say, "Math is my favorite subject, so I will study and master the skills in order to get good grades and make the honor roll." When you say this, your brain will go to work. You have programmed your brain to try.

Remember:

✓ The skills and concepts you master in school
will help you to succeed in life.

✓ People have different talents. Some people can swim, run, and kick
field goals, while others can cook, sing, and draw.

✓ Find your talents and interests. Work hard and practice them.
Then you will prove this author right.

ACTIVITY:

Make a pledge to be the best that you can be.

Repeat your pledge every day.

Set goals and work hard to reach them.

YOUR PLEDGE:

____

____

____

____

____

____

____

Never ever quit or give up on your dreams.
I believe in you. You are a winner! You are a Star!

When you believe in yourself, you can climb the highest
mountain, touch the bottom of the deepest sea, travel to
the ends of the earth, and **be the best that you can be!**

THUMBS UP! 

Lesson 26:
A Note From the Author
The Big Secret to Success! . . . Shhhhhh!

Many adults will confess to you that they had no idea what self-efficacy was when they were kids. They will also admit that if they understood self-efficacy, they would have achieved more in life. The truth is that *most people learn and understand self-efficacy concepts as adults*. Unfortunately, for some, it is too late since they already had a mediocre life and could not return to school to try again. Using self-efficacy to your advantage could determine how much money you make, what kind of home you own, and the car you can afford to drive later in life.

Your parents and teachers have many meetings about you. They discuss how to help you to be a success. Speaking honestly, I will tell you that they can discuss and plan all they want, but whether or not you succeed depends on your level of self-efficacy. The average kid does not want to think about being an adult while they are young, but you should understand that your childhood is a time when you build the foundation you will stand on later in life. People with poor self-efficacy will build a shaky, weak, and wobbly foundation that could fall apart during adulthood.

People with high self-efficacy build a firm foundation. They carry the same confident attitude throughout life. They become innovators, find their inner greatness, and become a success.

You could be this person.

The choice is all yours.

Let me summarize the big secret:

✓ People with high self-efficacy are not afraid to try new things.

✓ They do not give up after failing at something;
they just try again and again.

✓ They speak positive affirmations to themselves.

✓ When they fall, they pick themselves up
and do not wait for others to pick them up.

✓ They have an 'I can' attitude.

✓ They never say, "I can't."

✓ They know that the more they try,
the better their chance of succeeding.

Now you know the secret too.

People do not succeed and get rich by pure luck.
Instead, they work hard to achieve success and never give up.

THUMBS UP! 

Illustration ACTIVITY 1:
In the space below, draw a picture of Tony sitting on the
wall as described on pages 1-2 of the Mentor Text,
What You Say Is What You Are.

Explain your art. (What details helped you to visualize Tony's face?)

____

____

____

____

____

____

Lesson 27:

Illustration ACTIVITY 2:

In the space below, draw a picture of the scene on page 7 and 8
of the Mentor Text, *What You Say Is What You Are.*

Describe the details that helped you to visualize the picture you drew.

____

____

____

____

____

____

Lesson 28: Metaphors & Similes

ACTIVITY:

In your own words, explain what the title on page 11
means in the *What You Say Is What You Are,* Mentor Text.

____

____

____

____

A **metaphor** compares two things
by saying that one thing is another.

1. Reread page 7 from the Mentor Text. Find and write a metaphor.

____

____

2. Explain what the metaphor means.

____

____

3. Why do you think the author decided to compare these two things?

____

____

Think About It!

4. Why did it take Fred so long to get the message through to Andy?

____

____

A **visual** is the picture created in your mind as you read.

5. What pictures came to your mind as you read page 15?

____

____

6. Draw the image as you saw it in your mind.

7. What is your favorite visual from the Mentor Text?

____

____

8. Look back on pages 17-18 and make a prediction. What was Andy most likely saying to himself as he ran toward the school?

____

____

A **simile** compares two things using the words 'like or as'.

9. What is the simile on page 22?

____

____

10. What two things is the author comparing?

____

____

11. Why do you believe the author chose to compare these two things with one another?

____

____

12. Write the same simile but compare it to something else.

____

____

13. Write about a time when you felt like Andy felt on page 22. What happened?

____

____

14. How did you react?

____

____

15. What did you say to yourself?

____

____

16. If you could relive that moment, what would you do differently?

____

____

17. Write two positive attributes about yourself.

    1. _______________________________

    2. _______________________________

Lesson 29: Judgement
When you make a judgment, you decide how to react towards a person or situation.

ACTIVITY:

1. Make a judgment about Andy on page 23 of the storybook.

____

____

____

2. Andy made negative self-referent statements on page 25. The way Andy *thought* on page 32 is an example of this type of thinking. What type of thinking is this? Fill in the blanks.

__ __ __ __ __ __ __ __ __ __ thinking

3. Use context clues to determine the meaning of the word **mesmerized** on page 8 of the Mentor Text.

____

____

4. Use context clues to determine the meaning of the word **pensive** on page 41 of the Mentor Text.

____

____

A **theme** is the lesson in the story.

5. What is the theme of *What You Say Is What You Are,* Mentor Text?

____

____

____

6. What did you learn about yourself after reading *What You Say Is What You Are,* Mentor Text?

____

____

____

7. Explain what the title of the book means to you.

____

____

____

8. On a scale from 1 to 10, how would you rate your self-esteem **before you read** about Andy? Please circle your response below.

$$1 \quad 2 \quad 3 \quad 4 \quad 5 \quad 6 \quad 7 \quad 8 \quad 9 \quad 10$$

9. On a scale from 1 to 10, how would you rate your self-esteem *now* that you have read about Andy? Please circle your response below.

$$1 \quad 2 \quad 3 \quad 4 \quad 5 \quad 6 \quad 7 \quad 8 \quad 9 \quad 10$$

Lesson 30: Feelings Crossword Puzzle

More Emotion and Feeling Words

```
C Y V S K Q J P I A F D X D E
G I K G C S G D P W E U E A N
N Y T E U B D O D T X T E N R
I L J E U I L A E P A A D X A
V E C C H O L R S R A E D I G
O N D C G T M T T R T G O O E
L O X E J I A S Y N D H S U D
G L T U N G U P I B N J L S Q
L I Z E T R P O M F X G K A K
C Q D R F F P R N Y D X W P E
Z F Y J B P C D S W S B C D W
N U E S A G R D E Z I N O G A
G C H S D E K C O H S K A I I
H S I Q Q C G H Z B H L Z B R
S D N Y X I N L J Q A X B J M
```

AGONIZED	DISAPPOINTED	LONELY
ANXIOUS	ENRAGED	LOVING
APOLOGETIC	FRUSTRATED	SAD
DETERMINED	GUILTY	SHOCKED

ACTIVITY:

Write a poem about a winner. Please write at least two stanzas.

ACTIVITY:

Write a song about being positive and never giving up.

Lesson 31: Using Rational Thinking

DIRECTIONS: Complete the stories below by helping the characters use rational thinking skills. Please fill in the blanks using complete sentences.

A little girl named Angel loved to sing and dance, but she just could not sing on key or stay on beat. Angel, however, was great at drawing, so her friends often told her that she should forget about singing and dancing and focus on her drawing instead. Angel really enjoyed singing and dancing and always dreamed of being a superstar.

One day Angel competed in the school's talent show. She could tell that the people in the audience were not impressed with her act. It was time for Angel to make a decision. She thought about how much she loved to sing and dance and how well she could draw. Angel hated being laughed at. She finally made a decision to _______________

____

____

____

____

____

____

____

____

____

____

____

Rhijhaye was the fastest kid in his school. He proved it every day at recess, each time his peers challenged him in a race. There was always some kid trying to beat his record, but no one in the school could. Finally, field day was right around the corner, and Rhijhaye could hardly wait for his big moment to shine as his challengers got left behind in his dust.

One day a new student registered and joined Rhijhaye's class. His name was Tyhlr. He was tall and slinky, and his legs were three-quarters of his body height. Rhijhaye felt a lump rise in his throat as Tyhlr announced to the class that he was the fastest kid in his old school. During recess, all of the attention was taken away from Rhijhaye and given to Tyhlr, who won every race he was in. The kids all watched the two boys' big race on field day. It was close, but Tyhlr won. Rhijhaye felt ____

____

____

____

____

____

____

____

____

____

THUMBS UP! 

Lesson 32: Project 'Set Your Mind'

We are on a mission to teach every child how to develop a growth mindset through programming their minds for success. The first step is to identify and evaluate our personal character traits - those unique attributes and characteristics that define us as individuals. The second step will be to analyze the quality of our character traits to determine whether they are *help* agents or *hindering* agents. Finally, the third step will be actively exchanging those hindering traits for more helpful ones. This does not mean you have to become someone else. Rather, it means you will become a better version of yourself. The fourth step will be to, *set your mind* for success.

Sigmund Freud was an Austrian neurologist who, after years of research on human behavior, developed a theory of personality that explains how people view themselves as individuals. According to Mr. Freud, there are multiple versions of every person, two of which are the *actual* and *ideal* selves.

The **actual self** is the version we are in reality, while the **ideal self** is the version we wish we could be. The ideal version is the version we aspire to be because it is the best version of ourselves. For example, when we know an important event like a test is approaching, the actual version may choose to procrastinate, while the ideal version wants to prepare.

The problem is that whereas the actual self is the version who exists in reality, the ideal version exists only in our minds. So, the ideal version tells us to grab the book and study, but the actual version grabs the remote instead and promises to study right after you relax. Sounds familiar, right?

Now that this is making sense, let's move forward.

Since it is established that the less productive version of ourselves is the one with the physical control over our behavior, would it make sense for us to figure out a way to reverse this control and put the ideal version in charge?

You are absolutely right! Taking this action is an essential step in becoming the best that you can be. Let's discuss some character traits.

Examples of Character Traits:
Intrinsically-driven

Procrastinator

Respectful

Optimistic

Greedy

Jealous

Caring

Energetic

THUMBS UP! 

Lesson 33: Taking Steps to 'Set Your Mind'

STEP ONE:

Let's identify our character traits.

List your four most dominant character traits.

_______________________   _______________________

_______________________   _______________________

In order to be the best we can be, we must sometimes make decisions that go against how we actually feel. You may not feel like climbing the staircase, but if it's the only way to the top, you must make a decision to listen either to your actual-self version and walk away or obey the ideal version and begin the climb.

The actual-self version will often encourage you to take the easy path in whatever you have to do. Unfortunately, this path often leads to a less productive version of yourself. The truth is that becoming your ideal self takes *more* work and energy.

It requires you to practice more, try multiple times, experience disappointment, and even sometimes failure. Naturally, you will become frustrated at times and think about quitting. That is alright, because the most successful people you know also failed many times before they finally succeeded and became their best.

One of my favorite examples is Thomas Edison. You may know that he invented the light bulb, but did you know that before he succeeded, he had failed many times? See for yourself, by his very own confession during an interview when a reporter questioned him: "How did it feel to fail 1,000 times?"

Edison replied, "I didn't fail 1,000 times. The light bulb was an invention with 1,000 steps."[1] This response demonstrates Thomas Edison's rational thinking.

Some Famous Quotes About Trying Again After Failure:

"Ever tried. Ever failed. No matter. Try again. Fail again. Fail better."
-Samuel Beckett[2]

"Great success is built on failure, frustration, even catastrophe."
-Sumner Redstone[3]

"Only those who dare to fail greatly can achieve greatly."
-Robert F. Kennedy[4]

"Our greatest glory is not in never falling but in rising every time we fall."

-Confucius[5]

---

[1] "Thomas A. Edison Quotes." Quotefancy.com 23 January 2023
https://quotefancy.com/thomas-edison-quotes

[2] "Samuel Beckett Quotes." BrainyQuote.com. BrainyMedia Inc, 2023. 23 January 2023.
https://www.brainyquote.com/quotes/samuel_beckett_121335

[3] "Sumner Redstone Quotes." BrainyQuote.com. BrainyMedia Inc, 2023. 23 January 2023.
https://www.brainyquote.com/quotes/sumner_redstone_227812

[4] "Robert Kennedy Quotes." BrainyQuote.com. BrainyMedia Inc, 2023. 23 January 2023.
https://www.brainyquote.com/quotes/robert_kennedy_101795

[5] "Confucius Quotes." BrainyQuote.com. BrainyMedia Inc, 2023. 23 January 2023.
https://www.brainyquote.com/quotes/confucius_101164

Lesson 34: Help Agents or Hindering Agents?

ACTIVITY:

Are Your Character Traits Help Agents or Hindering Agents?

Let's consider person one, who has procrastination as a character trait. Person one constantly puts things off for a later time. The longer it takes to begin the task, the less time is allotted for the task to be completed. Therefore, this results in less time spent practicing and a greater chance of not mastering the task. This character trait is a hindrance to becoming the ideal version of oneself. At the end of it all, person one feels a sense of dissatisfaction and frustration from giving into the lethargic nature of the actual self.

Next, let's consider person two, who has perseverance as a character trait. Person two not only constantly practices a task but also has intrinsic energy that always tells them to keep trying. Person two begins tasks immediately, which provides extra time to perfect the task before the deadline. This results in a greater chance of mastering the task. This character trait is an example of a **help agent**. At the end of it all, person two feels satisfied and well accomplished for yielding to the driving nature of the ideal self.

STEP TWO:

Let's identify help agents and hindering agents.

Hindering agents are character traits that negatively affect your motivation to strive to be your very best. Remember, character traits that positively motivate you to strive for excellence are help agents.

Now, look back at your dominant character traits you identified on page 71 of this Activity Guide. These traits govern your life and control your motivation to succeed. Rewrite each of your traits in

Column One below and analyze them by writing hindering agent or help agent in Column Two.

Column One: **Column Two:**

_____________________   _____________________

_____________________   _____________________

_____________________   _____________________

_____________________   _____________________

If all of your character traits are help agents, you are on the right track to becoming the best you can be and the ideal version of yourself. However, if you discover that some of your traits are hindering agents, you first need to own them.

Accepting that you have weaknesses will help you to embrace the need to take the necessary actions to strengthen them and get on the path to becoming the best version of yourself.

THUMBS UP! 

Lesson 35: The 'Exchange Policy'

STEP THREE:

Let's learn about the 'Exchange Policy'.

Let's revisit person one in the scenario on page 73 of this Activity Guide. If this person makes no adjustments to the hindering agent of procrastination, then they may never grow to become the best version of who they could be. But what if person one decides to employ the exchange policy and trades the hindering agent for a help agent? After all, that is allowed. Exchanging procrastination for perseverance will enhance person one's chance of achieving true success.

But, is it really that easy to exchange character traits?

The truth is that it requires a serious commitment from you and one final step.

STEP FOUR:

Let's set our minds together.

Once you make the exchange for the help agent, the hindering agent will constantly attempt to get back in its original position. So, how do you prevent that from happening? You have to *set your mind.*

What does it mean to set your mind?

✓ It means that you make up your mind that you want to be the best you can be, and you will apply your best efforts to ensure you become the best version of yourself you can become.

✓ To set your mind means to make a conscious commitment to practice a task until you master it. It means that even when you get tired and want to give up, you decide to take away the control from your actual self and give the power to the ideal version of yourself. Setting your mind for success requires a key ingredient known as **determination**.

Positive Affirmation:

In a mirror, say to yourself:
I have only one option,
and that is to succeed.

Now, throw your fist in the air and chant with me:
Set my mind!
Set my mind!
Set my mind!
Then I'll win!

THUMBS UP! 

Lesson 36: How to Set Your Mind

At this point, you've been made aware of how entertaining irrational thoughts and beliefs can contribute to the development of learned helplessness and affect your self-efficacy. You are informed of the Freudian theory of the ideal versus actual versions of self and how each affects our academic drive and motivation. Therefore, you are now equipped to make a conscious decision about whether you will take the ideal path that leads to the best future version of yourself; or the alternative path which leads to a less ideal version of yourself.

Setting your mind isn't a one-time event. It's a repetitive process you consciously practice daily. Here is how it works:

- ✓ Each day, you remind yourself of your pledge to 'be the best that you can be, one moment at a time, one day at a time.'
- ✓ Then as you go through your day, approach each task with diligence, tenacity, and integrity. For example, if you are completing an assignment, do it to the best of your ability, even if no one is watching.
- ✓ Do your very best in every situation and never stop trying.
- ✓ Be willing to fail because, if you recall, that was a precursor to the success of many famous people who we look up to and admire. Unless they kept trying after they failed, they might never have succeeded.

QUESTION: Do you have what it takes?

- ❖ What type of people become successful?
- ❖ Is it only people who love school and would rather study than play?
- ❖ Is it exclusively people who are academically gifted and learning comes easy to them?

ANSWER: NO WAY!

Success is for anyone who wants it. Luck has little to do with success. In order to succeed at a goal, one must simply determine in their mind to put forth the necessary effort and practice.

Remember:

✓ The major difference between success
and failure is simply PRACTICE!

✓ YES! You do have what it takes to succeed
and be the best you can be.

Here is a quote from Lao Tzu which proves you can control your destiny by consciously applying the skills you have learned in the *What You Say Is What You Are,* Activity Guide:

"Watch your thoughts, they become your words;
watch your words, they become your actions;
watch your actions, they become your habits;
watch your habits, they become your character;
watch your character, it becomes your destiny."

-Lao Tzu[1]

---

[1] "Quotable Quote." Goodreads.com 24 January 2023
https://www.goodreads.com/quotes/8203490-watch-your-thoughts-they-become-your-words-watch-your-words

Lesson 37: Let's Review

This is your ♥ heart.

This is your 👄 mouth.

This is your 🧠 brain.

They are a very special team, communicating with each other every moment, even in your sleep.

Your mouth speaks whatever your heart believes. Your heart and brain believe whatever your mouth speaks.

So, from this moment forward, choose the right words to motivate your thoughts - to lead to such actions - that develop the most effective habits- that transform your character into alignment with your ideal destiny.

LAST WORD:
In your own words, describe what it means to set your mind for success.

____

____

____

____

____

What do you say?

It's time to decide. You are now fully equipped with the knowledge of how to become the best you can be, and the rest is completely up to you.

Sign the pledge below if you are ready to begin the journey of becoming the best you can be.

I, _________________, accept the challenge of applying the necessary effort and practice to become the ideal version of myself, to work hard at being the best that I can be, and to make my success a reality.

CONGRATULATIONS!

THUMBS UP! 

Additional Resources:

What you say is what you are.
You believe, and you'll go far.
If in your heart you do believe,
then I know you will achieve.

I can; I will; I believe; I am! (Repeat)

I believe it in my heart.
I can see it in my dreams.
It's imprinted in my mind.
I will succeed!

I had a vision.
I'm on a mission.
I've got passion for success.

I can! I will! I believe! I am!
I can! I will! I believe! I am!

(Repeat parts 1 and 2 above)

I say: I am a winner; I am the best!
     Give me a challenge; I know I'll pass that test.

I say: I'm a believer; I will achieve.
     Oh, it's not hard, cause I believe.

If I believe it and speak it, I will achieve it.
If I believe it and speak it, I will achieve it.
If I believe it and speak it, I will achieve it.
If I believe it and speak it!

What do you say?   I am confident, positive, and strong.
What do you say?   If I work hard, I can't go wrong.
What do you say?   My mind is as capable as any other.
What do you say?   I have the ability to be a Super Star!

I can!   I can be whatever I dream to be.
I will!   I'll be the best I can be one day at a time.
I believe!   I can train my brain to succeed.
I am!   That's Right!

I can! I will! I believe! I am!
I can! I will! I believe! I am!

Believe It! Speak It! Achieve It!
Whoooooo!   (Repeat 4x)

About the Author

Dr. Small is a children's advocate who stumbled upon a great phenomenon. Students who are made aware of SELF-EFFICACY and how to use it will boost their enthusiasm towards learning and life. Self-efficacy will produce a generation of exceptionally intelligent children and future favorable citizens.

> **Phenomenon:** Get students to want to learn. This will happen only when students begin to believe *they* can learn. Students who have unknowingly programmed their brains to fail need to be taught how to reset their minds to succeed. Some students have even tried to learn to no avail, because of a mental block toward learning, created by irrational thoughts. Being oblivious of this fact causes students to feel dumb and engage in negative self-referential statements such as, "I am stupid!" or "I am a loser!"

Students who repeatedly fail are usually unaware they are caught in a cycle *and* that cycle can be broken. Please help me in my efforts to open children's eyes to reveal to them the gift of intelligence within them.

This book will help bring students face-to-face with 'the power of self-talk'. Students will begin to understand they can control their actions with their words. The accompanying *What You Say Is What You Are Mentor Text* is a fictional story developed to show the principles shared in this Activity Guide. It follows the story of Andy resetting his mind to succeed. It effectively teaches children to use positive self-referential statements.

I embrace my mission to inspire children to become their best self, *One Moment At a Time* (OMAT). I believe, "These very children, regardless of how they approach this critical cycle, will grow up and be our future leaders and part of our communities Therefore, it behooves us to make them aware of how to apply self-talk as a tool to enhance motivation and enthusiasm toward learning and life. The alter-native is to allow them to grow up academically, socially, and psychologically unstable; ultimately becoming menaces to society and forfeiting their dreams."

As a teacher, I have taught my students that they have the ability to use their words to motivate their actions. That makes them superheroes and every superhero has power. Read the *Super-Hero Creed* below to learn how to activate your superpower.

Super-Hero Creed

I am a Super-Hero! I make good things happen! I have word-power, and *negative* words are my kryptonite! I know that *positive* words are the fuel that energizes me and restores my strength!

I can use my word-power to block irrational thoughts that cause low self-esteem! With the POWER-4 process as my shield, I can set my mind to succeed!

If I believe it, speak it, and practice it, I can achieve anything I put my mind to! I acknowledge I am the most powerful type of Super-Hero because I have the power to train my brain and therefore, control my actions. I am a Super-Hero.

-Watch me soar!

For additional resources or to contact the author, please send correspondence to:

contactdrsmall@gmail.com

Or by mail: PO Box 210832

Royal Palm Beach, FL 33411

Dr. Small is available for author talks, book signings, professional development, workshops, and presentations.

Our team will conduct workshops to teach your team how to implement our *Character Circle* in your school using the *What You Say Is What You Are Mentor Text, Activity Guide*, and *Character Chant Audio* learning resources.

Page 29: My Emotions and Feelings are Important Solution

```
D S D + + + + + A + + + E D D
E D U A T + + N + D + L + E E
N E + O S N G + E + B + C I S
E V + + I R E X + A + O + F S
T E + + Y C E R R + N + J S A
H I D + + L I E E F + E H I R
G L + E P + S P I F A + U T R
I E + R T I + D S L F + R A A
R R E + M S E + O U + I T S B
F P + + D N U U + + S + D + M
+ + + + T A S G D E R O B N E
H A P P Y + M + S + + + + + I
L U F E T A R G + I + + + + +
+ + + + + + + + + D + + + +
+ + + + + + + + + + + + + +
```

```
(Over, Down, Direction)
ANGRY(9,1,SW)
BORED(13,11,W)
CONFIDENT(13,3,SW)
DISGUSTED(11,14,NW)
EMBARRASSED(15,11,N)
FRIGHTENED(1,10,N)
GRATEFUL(8,13,W)
HAPPY(1,12,E)
HURT(13,6,S)
INDIFFERENT(15,12,NW)
JEALOUS(13,5,SW)
MAD(7,12,NW)
MISERABLE(5,9,NE)
PERPLEXED(2,10,NE)
RELIEVED(2,9,N)
SAD(5,3,NW)
SATISFIED(14,9,N)
SUSPICIOUS(11,10,NW)
```

Page 60:

1. Metaphor: She is a flash with feet.
2. It means that Donna is so fast that she reminds you of how fast a flash comes out of a camera.
3. To get the reader to visualize just how fast Donna was.
4. Because Andy had programmed his brain to only believe negative statements, and that's all he could hear.

Page 61:

9. The simile sentence: In an instant . . .

Page 62:

10 The author compares the speed of Dave's words to the
   speed of a freight train.

Page 63:

2. Irrational

3. Mesmerize: see dictionary

4. Pensive: see dictionary

Page 64:

5. Theme: Believe in yourself and you can achieve anything at all.

Page 65:

More Emotion and Feeling Words Solution

```
C + + + + + + + A + D + D E
G I + G + + + P + E + E A N
N Y T + U + D O + T + T + N R
I L + E + I L A E + A + D X A
V E + + H O L R S R + E + I G
O N + + G T M T T + T + + O E
L O + E + I A S Y N + + + U D
+ L T + N + U P I + + + + S +
+ I + E + R + O M + + + + + +
C + D + F + P + + Y + + + + +
+ + + + + P + + + S + + + +
+ + + + A + + D E Z I N O G A
+ + + S D E K C O H S + + + +
+ + 1 + + + + + + + + + + +
+ D + + + + + + + + + + + +
```

(Over, Down, Direction)
AGONIZED(15,12,W)
ANXIOUS(14,2,S)
APOLOGETIC(10,1,SW)
DETERMINED(12,1,SW)
DISAPPOINTED(2,15,NE)
ENRAGED(15,1,S)
FRUSTRATED(5,10,NE)
GUILTY(4,2,SE)
LONELY(2,8,N)
LOVING(1,7,N)
SAD(9,5,NW)
SHOCKED(11,13,W)
SYMPATHETIC(11,11,NW)

www.ingramcontent.com/pod-product-compliance
Lightning Source LLC
Chambersburg PA
CBHW080338030726
47594CB00011B/4073